Here I Am, God

Copyright © 1990 Éditions du Centurion/Bayard Presse
Translation copyright © 1991 Lion Publishing plc

Published by
Lion Publishing plc
Sandy Lane West, Oxford, England
ISBN 0 7459 1960 X
Lion Publishing Corporation
1705 Hubbard Avenue, Batavia, Illinois 60510, USA
ISBN 0 7459 1960 X
Albatross Books Pty Ltd
PO Box 320, Sutherland, NSW 2232, Australia
ISBN 0 7324 0266 2

First published 1990 by Éditions du Centurion/Bayard Presse under the title
of *Images pour prier de tout son corps*
First English edition published 1991 by Lion Publishing plc

British Library CIP data and Library of Congress CIP data applied for

Printed in France
Impression et reliure : Pollina s.a., 85400 Luçon - n° 13177

My Picture Prayer Book

Here I Am, God

Marie-Agnès Gaudrat
Illustrations by Letizia Galli

A LION BOOK

Oxford · Batavia · Sydney

Preface

We all use "body language"—actions and gestures—when we talk. Children use body language quite naturally and spontaneously: little ones who cannot express their feelings in words show they are happy by dancing on the spot or waving their hands in the air; when they are sad or cross, their mood is reflected in their faces and their bodies. Older children continue to reinforce what they are saying or thinking with gestures and actions—and sometimes actions do "speak louder than words".

Prayer is expressing a relationship with God. Christians from different church traditions may stand, sit, kneel or even lie down to pray. They may raise their hands. They may sway or dance. As the Bible reveals, prayer involves the whole person— body, mind and spirit—all at once. It also shows that we are individuals guided, inspired and loved by God, to whom he has given life, breath and feelings.

Children, especially, are aware of their bodies, without the limits which adults all too readily set themselves. So it is natural and right for children to express every part of themselves when they pray. This book is especially designed to help them enjoy this freedom to come before God just as they are. The pages at the end of the book explain how it works and suggest how to use it.

Prayer is like running towards God

When you run towards someone
it's because you really want to.
You don't think about it,
you don't hesitate,
you just run.
You are not running towards the unknown,
but towards someone who loves you
and welcomes you with open arms.

The next three pictures
are to help you talk to God.
They show that the way we come to God
says as much as the words
that we use to pray
—and perhaps even more.

Thank you

I'm glad I can eat,
I can breathe, rest and play;
I'm glad I have parents who love me.
But most of all,
I'm glad I'm alive
to enjoy today!

*Dear God, I lift my hands to you
in joyful thanks.*

Sorry

I don't like the things I've done
and now I don't like me.
It's as if I'm sitting at the bottom
of a ditch, as gloomy as can be.
Does anyone love me enough
to help me to like myself again?

*Dear God, I'm sitting in a heap.
Look at me, you can see that
I'm sorry.*

Hello

I'm not too proud, I'm not ashamed,
no need to hide my face.
I'm standing here, just as I am
in my own little space.

Hello, God,
I like being here with you,
like a child with its father.

Prayer is like being hugged by God

When someone you love gives you a hug,
you feel really safe.
You can talk or just say nothing
and still be sure
that you really are loved.

But sometimes you don't want a hug
because you feel bad inside,
or because you feel cross and bothered.
Sometimes when you feel like this
you can't pray to God.

On the next three pages
there are three pictures
to help you pray
when you don't feel like praying.

Opening your hands

There are days
when you feel sulky and cross.
On those days
you can help yourself to pray
by just sitting down
and opening your hands,
a bit like opening the windows
of a gloomy, locked-up house
to let the sunshine
and the fresh air in.

*Opening my hands in prayer
is another way of saying,
"Dear God, come in, come into
my house."*

Curling up in a ball

Some days,
you just can't stop thinking
about all the things you've done,
about what you're going to do,
about everything, in fact,
except praying.
It's a bit like
asking someone to visit you,
then going out instead.
On those days
you can curl up
in a ball
and quietly make
a space inside
where you can
meet with God.

When I curl up to pray
it's a bit like saying to God,
"You can come—I'm waiting here."

Rocking

Sometimes
you feel so wriggly
that you can't sit still.
On those days,
when you want to pray,
stand on one foot,
gently sway
back to the other,
as if you are a child
cradled in God's arms.

Rocking gently when I pray
is another way of saying,
"Dear God, please hold me close."

Prayer is like giving God a present

When you give someone a present
it's because they're special to you.
When you give them something
you've made,
you know you can trust them
not to laugh at it
but to treasure it.

Did you know
that you are just as special to God?
Praying isn't just
about hands together, eyes closed.
Prayer is also about
showing God the things you've done,
the things you've made.

The next three pictures
are to help you pray
by giving God what you do,
what you make
and what you are.

Making things

My hands can do so many things.
I can draw pictures and I can write.
I can make models.
I can push and pull and catch.
I can build and make all kinds
of things.

*When I use my hands
to make something,
I think of you, dear God,
the maker of all things.*

Walking

Here I stand
with my feet on the ground.
I stand on one foot, then the other,
I can walk, I can run,
I can jump, I can dance.

When I walk,
I think of you, dear God,
leading me along.

Holding hands

I like holding hands.
It makes me feel safe
to have someone beside me
wherever I go.
I know I can't get lost when I'm
holding hands.

When I hold someone's hand
I think of you, dear God,
as you walk beside me day by day.

Prayer is like a seed

You can't tell by looking
when a seed first starts to grow.
But, hidden in the earth,
it sprouts and grows into a plant
with leaves and fruit.

Praying is like letting
a little bit of God
grow within us.

The next three pictures
are to show
how our mouths, our eyes, and our hands
can make our prayers
like plants which grow and bear fruit.

My mouth

My mouth
can be spiteful,
my mouth can be kind,
it can speak words of hate
or of love.
It can bite, it can kiss,
it can tell lies,
or it can tell the truth.

*Today I want to use
my mouth to speak the truth.
This is my prayer, dear God.*

My eyes

I can look around and see
everything that's going on.
I can see that I belong
in the world.
I can open my eyes wide
and see God's world on every side.
I can close them tight
and shut out the rest of the world.

*I want to open my eyes
and see where I belong.
This is my prayer, dear God.*

My hands

I can hold my hands
in a fist
to hit and hurt and hate.
Or I can gently stroke
and soothe
and take the hurt away.

*I want to use my hands
in gentle ways.
This is my prayer, dear God.*

Prayer is belonging

Prayer joins us together
with a great family of people
who believe in God.
When you pray,
even when you are all alone,
you are part of the family:
people of the present
—around the world today—
and people of the past.

The next three pictures are for you
to look at as you say again words
used by other people
who believed in God long ago.

You make me sure-footed

You make me
sure-footed as a deer;
You keep me
safe on the mountain.

From Psalm 18

*Dear God, you show me
the way to go and give me
a wide path to walk along.*

Looking to you

Those who look to you,
dear God,
need never be afraid.
Those who look to you,
dear God,
need never feel ashamed.

Psalm 34:5

Dear God, I look to you.

Like a child

Dear God, please look at me,
my heart is not proud.
Dear God, please look at me,
I am now still and quiet.
Dear God, please look at me,
I am like a child
in its mother's arms.

Psalm 131

Dear God, when I am with you,
I am like a child
in its mother's arms.

How this book works

Section 1: Children use body language naturally. Here are three pictures to help them pray according to how they are feeling: **thank you**, page 8; **sorry,** page 10; **hello, God,** page 12.

Section 2: Children find it hard to sit still. Here are three pictures to help them find a physical way of starting their prayers: **opening your hands,** page 16; **curling up in a ball,** page 18; **rocking,** page 20.

Section 3: What is God like, and what kind of prayers is it right to use? Each person's answer will be different. Sometimes you will kneel to pray, and at others you will pray as you walk along. Here are three pictures to help children pray in relation to their daily lives: **making things,** page 24; **walking,** page 26; **holding hands,** page 28.

Section 4: Children's prayers are often inspired by everyday life. They do not naturally see that it can work the other way; that prayer can inspire their everyday life. Here are three pictures to help them: **my mouth,** page 32; **my eyes,** page 34; **my hands,** page 36.

Section 5: Prayer also links the person who prays to the rest of the "family of God". Here are three pictures which show that, in the psalms of the Old

Testament, meeting God in prayer is expressed in physical terms: **you make me sure-footed,** page 40; **looking to you,** page 42; **like a child,** page 44.

How to use this book with children

The simplest way is to work through the book from beginning to end, stopping to look and read where the child shows interest. Or you might like to use a picture from section two to help your child start to pray.

Yet another way would be to dip into it regularly, using a familiar, relevant starting-point. For example, after a long walk you could select the prayer about "walking". After a day with a special friend, the prayer about "holding hands" may strike a chord. A child who feels hurt and upset after an argument may be reassured by the prayer "sorry".

Gradually, children will learn to use the picture that matches their mood or the occasion. If the picture inspires other prayers, or just quiet thought, that is fine. Children should feel to feel free to talk to God without any inhibitions. This book is a starting-point to help them do this.